Cryptocurrency Trader's Portfolio

JAMES F. HATCHER III

ISBN-13: 978-1981763146
ISBN-10: 1981763147

Available from Amazon.com, CreateSpace.com,
and other retail outlets.

Published by The Masonic Press.
Find more interesting titles on our website:

masonicpress.com

Printed by CreateSpace, Charleston, SC
An Amazon.com Company

COIN/TOKEN:_____ Exchange:_____

DATE	BUY @ PRICE	BUY AMOUNT	MIN SELL PT	SELL @ PRICE	SELL AMOUNT	PROFIT/LOSS

COIN/TOKEN:_____ Exchange:_____

DATE	BUY @ PRICE	BUY AMOUNT	MIN SELL PT	SELL @ PRICE	SELL AMOUNT	PROFIT/LOSS

COIN/TOKEN:_____ Exchange:_____

DATE	BUY @ PRICE	BUY AMOUNT	MIN SELL PT	SELL @ PRICE	SELL AMOUNT	PROFIT/LOSS

COIN/TOKEN:_____ Exchange:_____

DATE	BUY @ PRICE	BUY AMOUNT	MIN SELL PT	SELL @ PRICE	SELL AMOUNT	PROFIT/LOSS

COIN/TOKEN:_____ Exchange:_____

DATE	BUY @ PRICE	BUY AMOUNT	MIN SELL PT	SELL @ PRICE	SELL AMOUNT	PROFIT/LOSS

COIN/TOKEN:_____ Exchange:_____

DATE	BUY @ PRICE	BUY AMOUNT	MIN SELL PT	SELL @ PRICE	SELL AMOUNT	PROFIT/LOSS

COIN/TOKEN:_____ Exchange:_____

DATE	BUY @ PRICE	BUY AMOUNT	MIN SELL PT	SELL @ PRICE	SELL AMOUNT	PROFIT/LOSS

COIN/TOKEN:_____ Exchange:_____

DATE	BUY @ PRICE	BUY AMOUNT	MIN SELL PT	SELL @ PRICE	SELL AMOUNT	PROFIT/LOSS

COIN/TOKEN:_____ Exchange:_____

DATE	BUY @ PRICE	BUY AMOUNT	MIN SELL PT	SELL @ PRICE	SELL AMOUNT	PROFIT/LOSS

COIN/TOKEN:_____ Exchange:_____

DATE	BUY @ PRICE	BUY AMOUNT	MIN SELL PT	SELL @ PRICE	SELL AMOUNT	PROFIT/LOSS

COIN/TOKEN:_____ Exchange:_____

DATE	BUY @ PRICE	BUY AMOUNT	MIN SELL PT	SELL @ PRICE	SELL AMOUNT	PROFIT/LOSS

COIN/TOKEN:_____ Exchange:_____

DATE	BUY @ PRICE	BUY AMOUNT	MIN SELL PT	SELL @ PRICE	SELL AMOUNT	PROFIT/LOSS

COIN/TOKEN:_____ Exchange:_____

DATE	BUY @ PRICE	BUY AMOUNT	MIN SELL PT	SELL @ PRICE	SELL AMOUNT	PROFIT/LOSS

COIN/TOKEN:_____ Exchange:_____

DATE	BUY @ PRICE	BUY AMOUNT	MIN SELL PT	SELL @ PRICE	SELL AMOUNT	PROFIT/LOSS

COIN/TOKEN:_____ Exchange:_____

DATE	BUY @ PRICE	BUY AMOUNT	MIN SELL PT	SELL @ PRICE	SELL AMOUNT	PROFIT/LOSS

COIN/TOKEN:_____ Exchange:_____

DATE	BUY @ PRICE	BUY AMOUNT	MIN SELL PT	SELL @ PRICE	SELL AMOUNT	PROFIT/LOSS

COIN/TOKEN:_____ Exchange:_____

DATE	BUY @ PRICE	BUY AMOUNT	MIN SELL PT	SELL @ PRICE	SELL AMOUNT	PROFIT/LOSS

COIN/TOKEN:_____ Exchange:_____

DATE	BUY @ PRICE	BUY AMOUNT	MIN SELL PT	SELL @ PRICE	SELL AMOUNT	PROFIT/LOSS

COIN/TOKEN:_____ Exchange:_____

DATE	BUY @ PRICE	BUY AMOUNT	MIN SELL PT	SELL @ PRICE	SELL AMOUNT	PROFIT/LOSS

COIN/TOKEN:_____ Exchange:_____

DATE	BUY @ PRICE	BUY AMOUNT	MIN SELL PT	SELL @ PRICE	SELL AMOUNT	PROFIT/LOSS

COIN/TOKEN:_____ Exchange:_____

DATE	BUY @ PRICE	BUY AMOUNT	MIN SELL PT	SELL @ PRICE	SELL AMOUNT	PROFIT/LOSS

COIN/TOKEN:_____ Exchange:_____

DATE	BUY @ PRICE	BUY AMOUNT	MIN SELL PT	SELL @ PRICE	SELL AMOUNT	PROFIT/LOSS

COIN/TOKEN:_____ Exchange:_____

DATE	BUY @ PRICE	BUY AMOUNT	MIN SELL PT	SELL @ PRICE	SELL AMOUNT	PROFIT/LOSS

COIN/TOKEN:_____ Exchange:_____

DATE	BUY @ PRICE	BUY AMOUNT	MIN SELL PT	SELL @ PRICE	SELL AMOUNT	PROFIT/LOSS

COIN/TOKEN:_____ Exchange:_____

DATE	BUY @ PRICE	BUY AMOUNT	MIN SELL PT	SELL @ PRICE	SELL AMOUNT	PROFIT/LOSS

COIN/TOKEN:_____ Exchange:_____

DATE	BUY @ PRICE	BUY AMOUNT	MIN SELL PT	SELL @ PRICE	SELL AMOUNT	PROFIT/LOSS

COIN/TOKEN:_____ Exchange:_____

DATE	BUY @ PRICE	BUY AMOUNT	MIN SELL PT	SELL @ PRICE	SELL AMOUNT	PROFIT/LOSS

COIN/TOKEN:_____ Exchange:_____

DATE	BUY @ PRICE	BUY AMOUNT	MIN SELL PT	SELL @ PRICE	SELL AMOUNT	PROFIT/LOSS

COIN/TOKEN:_____ Exchange:_____

DATE	BUY @ PRICE	BUY AMOUNT	MIN SELL PT	SELL @ PRICE	SELL AMOUNT	PROFIT/LOSS

COIN/TOKEN:_____ Exchange:_____

DATE	BUY @ PRICE	BUY AMOUNT	MIN SELL PT	SELL @ PRICE	SELL AMOUNT	PROFIT/LOSS

COIN/TOKEN:_____ Exchange:_____

DATE	BUY @ PRICE	BUY AMOUNT	MIN SELL PT	SELL @ PRICE	SELL AMOUNT	PROFIT/LOSS

COIN/TOKEN:_____ Exchange:_____

DATE	BUY @ PRICE	BUY AMOUNT	MIN SELL PT	SELL @ PRICE	SELL AMOUNT	PROFIT/LOSS

COIN/TOKEN:_____ Exchange:_____

DATE	BUY @ PRICE	BUY AMOUNT	MIN SELL PT	SELL @ PRICE	SELL AMOUNT	PROFIT/LOSS

COIN/TOKEN:_____ Exchange:_____

DATE	BUY @ PRICE	BUY AMOUNT	MIN SELL PT	SELL @ PRICE	SELL AMOUNT	PROFIT/LOSS

COIN/TOKEN:_____ Exchange:_____

DATE	BUY @ PRICE	BUY AMOUNT	MIN SELL PT	SELL @ PRICE	SELL AMOUNT	PROFIT/LOSS

COIN/TOKEN:_____ Exchange:_____

DATE	BUY @ PRICE	BUY AMOUNT	MIN SELL PT	SELL @ PRICE	SELL AMOUNT	PROFIT/LOSS

COIN/TOKEN:_____ Exchange:_____

DATE	BUY @ PRICE	BUY AMOUNT	MIN SELL PT	SELL @ PRICE	SELL AMOUNT	PROFIT/LOSS

COIN/TOKEN:_____ Exchange:_____

DATE	BUY @ PRICE	BUY AMOUNT	MIN SELL PT	SELL @ PRICE	SELL AMOUNT	PROFIT/LOSS

COIN/TOKEN:_____ Exchange:_____

DATE	BUY @ PRICE	BUY AMOUNT	MIN SELL PT	SELL @ PRICE	SELL AMOUNT	PROFIT/LOSS

COIN/TOKEN:_____ Exchange:_____

DATE	BUY @ PRICE	BUY AMOUNT	MIN SELL PT	SELL @ PRICE	SELL AMOUNT	PROFIT/LOSS

COIN/TOKEN:_____ Exchange:_____

DATE	BUY @ PRICE	BUY AMOUNT	MIN SELL PT	SELL @ PRICE	SELL AMOUNT	PROFIT/LOSS

COIN/TOKEN:_____ Exchange:_____

DATE	BUY @ PRICE	BUY AMOUNT	MIN SELL PT	SELL @ PRICE	SELL AMOUNT	PROFIT/LOSS

COIN/TOKEN:_____ Exchange:_____

DATE	BUY @ PRICE	BUY AMOUNT	MIN SELL PT	SELL @ PRICE	SELL AMOUNT	PROFIT/LOSS

COIN/TOKEN:_____ Exchange:_____

DATE	BUY @ PRICE	BUY AMOUNT	MIN SELL PT	SELL @ PRICE	SELL AMOUNT	PROFIT/LOSS

COIN/TOKEN:_____ Exchange:_____

DATE	BUY @ PRICE	BUY AMOUNT	MIN SELL PT	SELL @ PRICE	SELL AMOUNT	PROFIT/LOSS

COIN/TOKEN:_____ Exchange:_____

DATE	BUY @ PRICE	BUY AMOUNT	MIN SELL PT	SELL @ PRICE	SELL AMOUNT	PROFIT/LOSS

COIN/TOKEN:_____ Exchange:_____

DATE	BUY @ PRICE	BUY AMOUNT	MIN SELL PT	SELL @ PRICE	SELL AMOUNT	PROFIT/LOSS

COIN/TOKEN:_____ Exchange:_____

DATE	BUY @ PRICE	BUY AMOUNT	MIN SELL PT	SELL @ PRICE	SELL AMOUNT	PROFIT/LOSS

COIN/TOKEN:_____ Exchange:_____

DATE	BUY @ PRICE	BUY AMOUNT	MIN SELL PT	SELL @ PRICE	SELL AMOUNT	PROFIT/LOSS

COIN/TOKEN:_____ Exchange:_____

DATE	BUY @ PRICE	BUY AMOUNT	MIN SELL PT	SELL @ PRICE	SELL AMOUNT	PROFIT/LOSS

COIN/TOKEN:_____ Exchange:_____

DATE	BUY @ PRICE	BUY AMOUNT	MIN SELL PT	SELL @ PRICE	SELL AMOUNT	PROFIT/LOSS

COIN/TOKEN:_____ Exchange:_____

DATE	BUY @ PRICE	BUY AMOUNT	MIN SELL PT	SELL @ PRICE	SELL AMOUNT	PROFIT/LOSS

COIN/TOKEN:_____ Exchange:_____

DATE	BUY @ PRICE	BUY AMOUNT	MIN SELL PT	SELL @ PRICE	SELL AMOUNT	PROFIT/LOSS

COIN/TOKEN:_____ Exchange:_____

DATE	BUY @ PRICE	BUY AMOUNT	MIN SELL PT	SELL @ PRICE	SELL AMOUNT	PROFIT/LOSS

COIN/TOKEN:_____ Exchange:_____

DATE	BUY @ PRICE	BUY AMOUNT	MIN SELL PT	SELL @ PRICE	SELL AMOUNT	PROFIT/LOSS

COIN/TOKEN:_____ Exchange:_____

DATE	BUY @ PRICE	BUY AMOUNT	MIN SELL PT	SELL @ PRICE	SELL AMOUNT	PROFIT/LOSS

COIN/TOKEN:_____ Exchange:_____

DATE	BUY @ PRICE	BUY AMOUNT	MIN SELL PT	SELL @ PRICE	SELL AMOUNT	PROFIT/LOSS

COIN/TOKEN:_____ Exchange:_____

DATE	BUY @ PRICE	BUY AMOUNT	MIN SELL PT	SELL @ PRICE	SELL AMOUNT	PROFIT/LOSS

COIN/TOKEN:_____ Exchange:_____

DATE	BUY @ PRICE	BUY AMOUNT	MIN SELL PT	SELL @ PRICE	SELL AMOUNT	PROFIT/LOSS

COIN/TOKEN:_____ Exchange:_____

DATE	BUY @ PRICE	BUY AMOUNT	MIN SELL PT	SELL @ PRICE	SELL AMOUNT	PROFIT/LOSS

COIN/TOKEN:_____ Exchange:_____

DATE	BUY @ PRICE	BUY AMOUNT	MIN SELL PT	SELL @ PRICE	SELL AMOUNT	PROFIT/LOSS

COIN/TOKEN:_____ Exchange:_____

DATE	BUY @ PRICE	BUY AMOUNT	MIN SELL PT	SELL @ PRICE	SELL AMOUNT	PROFIT/LOSS

COIN/TOKEN:_____ Exchange:_____

DATE	BUY @ PRICE	BUY AMOUNT	MIN SELL PT	SELL @ PRICE	SELL AMOUNT	PROFIT/LOSS

COIN/TOKEN:_____ Exchange:_____

DATE	BUY @ PRICE	BUY AMOUNT	MIN SELL PT	SELL @ PRICE	SELL AMOUNT	PROFIT/LOSS

COIN/TOKEN:_____ Exchange:_____

DATE	BUY @ PRICE	BUY AMOUNT	MIN SELL PT	SELL @ PRICE	SELL AMOUNT	PROFIT/LOSS

COIN/TOKEN:_____ Exchange:_____

DATE	BUY @ PRICE	BUY AMOUNT	MIN SELL PT	SELL @ PRICE	SELL AMOUNT	PROFIT/LOSS

COIN/TOKEN:_____ Exchange:_____

DATE	BUY @ PRICE	BUY AMOUNT	MIN SELL PT	SELL @ PRICE	SELL AMOUNT	PROFIT/LOSS

COIN/TOKEN:_____ Exchange:_____

DATE	BUY @ PRICE	BUY AMOUNT	MIN SELL PT	SELL @ PRICE	SELL AMOUNT	PROFIT/LOSS

COIN/TOKEN:_____ Exchange:_____

DATE	BUY @ PRICE	BUY AMOUNT	MIN SELL PT	SELL @ PRICE	SELL AMOUNT	PROFIT/LOSS

COIN/TOKEN:_____ Exchange:_____

DATE	BUY @ PRICE	BUY AMOUNT	MIN SELL PT	SELL @ PRICE	SELL AMOUNT	PROFIT/LOSS

COIN/TOKEN:_____ Exchange:_____

DATE	BUY @ PRICE	BUY AMOUNT	MIN SELL PT	SELL @ PRICE	SELL AMOUNT	PROFIT/LOSS

COIN/TOKEN:_____ Exchange:_____

DATE	BUY @ PRICE	BUY AMOUNT	MIN SELL PT	SELL @ PRICE	SELL AMOUNT	PROFIT/LOSS

COIN/TOKEN:_____ Exchange:_____

DATE	BUY @ PRICE	BUY AMOUNT	MIN SELL PT	SELL @ PRICE	SELL AMOUNT	PROFIT/LOSS

COIN/TOKEN:_____ Exchange:_____

DATE	BUY @ PRICE	BUY AMOUNT	MIN SELL PT	SELL @ PRICE	SELL AMOUNT	PROFIT/LOSS

COIN/TOKEN:_____ Exchange:_____

DATE	BUY @ PRICE	BUY AMOUNT	MIN SELL PT	SELL @ PRICE	SELL AMOUNT	PROFIT/LOSS

COIN/TOKEN:_____ Exchange:_____

DATE	BUY @ PRICE	BUY AMOUNT	MIN SELL PT	SELL @ PRICE	SELL AMOUNT	PROFIT/LOSS

COIN/TOKEN:_____ Exchange:_____

DATE	BUY @ PRICE	BUY AMOUNT	MIN SELL PT	SELL @ PRICE	SELL AMOUNT	PROFIT/LOSS

COIN/TOKEN:_____ Exchange:_____

DATE	BUY @ PRICE	BUY AMOUNT	MIN SELL PT	SELL @ PRICE	SELL AMOUNT	PROFIT/LOSS

COIN/TOKEN:_____ Exchange:_____

DATE	BUY @ PRICE	BUY AMOUNT	MIN SELL PT	SELL @ PRICE	SELL AMOUNT	PROFIT/LOSS

COIN/TOKEN:_____ Exchange:_____

DATE	BUY @ PRICE	BUY AMOUNT	MIN SELL PT	SELL @ PRICE	SELL AMOUNT	PROFIT/LOSS

COIN/TOKEN:_____ Exchange:_____

DATE	BUY @ PRICE	BUY AMOUNT	MIN SELL PT	SELL @ PRICE	SELL AMOUNT	PROFIT/LOSS

COIN/TOKEN:_____ Exchange:_____

DATE	BUY @ PRICE	BUY AMOUNT	MIN SELL PT	SELL @ PRICE	SELL AMOUNT	PROFIT/LOSS

COIN/TOKEN:_____ Exchange:_____

DATE	BUY @ PRICE	BUY AMOUNT	MIN SELL PT	SELL @ PRICE	SELL AMOUNT	PROFIT/LOSS

COIN/TOKEN:_____ Exchange:_____

DATE	BUY @ PRICE	BUY AMOUNT	MIN SELL PT	SELL @ PRICE	SELL AMOUNT	PROFIT/LOSS

COIN/TOKEN:_____ Exchange:_____

DATE	BUY @ PRICE	BUY AMOUNT	MIN SELL PT	SELL @ PRICE	SELL AMOUNT	PROFIT/LOSS

COIN/TOKEN:_____ Exchange:_____

DATE	BUY @ PRICE	BUY AMOUNT	MIN SELL PT	SELL @ PRICE	SELL AMOUNT	PROFIT/LOSS

COIN/TOKEN:_____ Exchange:_____

DATE	BUY @ PRICE	BUY AMOUNT	MIN SELL PT	SELL @ PRICE	SELL AMOUNT	PROFIT/LOSS

COIN/TOKEN:_____ Exchange:_____

DATE	BUY @ PRICE	BUY AMOUNT	MIN SELL PT	SELL @ PRICE	SELL AMOUNT	PROFIT/LOSS

COIN/TOKEN:_____ Exchange:_____

DATE	BUY @ PRICE	BUY AMOUNT	MIN SELL PT	SELL @ PRICE	SELL AMOUNT	PROFIT/LOSS

COIN/TOKEN:_____ Exchange:_____

DATE	BUY @ PRICE	BUY AMOUNT	MIN SELL PT	SELL @ PRICE	SELL AMOUNT	PROFIT/LOSS

COIN/TOKEN:_____ Exchange:_____

DATE	BUY @ PRICE	BUY AMOUNT	MIN SELL PT	SELL @ PRICE	SELL AMOUNT	PROFIT/LOSS

COIN/TOKEN:_____ Exchange:_____

DATE	BUY @ PRICE	BUY AMOUNT	MIN SELL PT	SELL @ PRICE	SELL AMOUNT	PROFIT/LOSS

COIN/TOKEN:_____ Exchange:_____

DATE	BUY @ PRICE	BUY AMOUNT	MIN SELL PT	SELL @ PRICE	SELL AMOUNT	PROFIT/LOSS

COIN/TOKEN:_____ Exchange:_____

DATE	BUY @ PRICE	BUY AMOUNT	MIN SELL PT	SELL @ PRICE	SELL AMOUNT	PROFIT/LOSS

COIN/TOKEN:_____ Exchange:_____

DATE	BUY @ PRICE	BUY AMOUNT	MIN SELL PT	SELL @ PRICE	SELL AMOUNT	PROFIT/LOSS

COIN/TOKEN:_____ Exchange:_____

DATE	BUY @ PRICE	BUY AMOUNT	MIN SELL PT	SELL @ PRICE	SELL AMOUNT	PROFIT/LOSS

COIN/TOKEN:_____ Exchange:_____

DATE	BUY @ PRICE	BUY AMOUNT	MIN SELL PT	SELL @ PRICE	SELL AMOUNT	PROFIT/LOSS

COIN/TOKEN:_____ Exchange:_____

DATE	BUY @ PRICE	BUY AMOUNT	MIN SELL PT	SELL @ PRICE	SELL AMOUNT	PROFIT/LOSS

COIN/TOKEN:_____ Exchange:_____

DATE	BUY @ PRICE	BUY AMOUNT	MIN SELL PT	SELL @ PRICE	SELL AMOUNT	PROFIT/LOSS

COIN/TOKEN:_____ Exchange:_____

DATE	BUY @ PRICE	BUY AMOUNT	MIN SELL PT	SELL @ PRICE	SELL AMOUNT	PROFIT/LOSS

COIN/TOKEN:_____ Exchange:_____

DATE	BUY @ PRICE	BUY AMOUNT	MIN SELL PT	SELL @ PRICE	SELL AMOUNT	PROFIT/LOSS

COIN/TOKEN:_____ Exchange:_____

DATE	BUY @ PRICE	BUY AMOUNT	MIN SELL PT	SELL @ PRICE	SELL AMOUNT	PROFIT/LOSS

COIN/TOKEN:_____ Exchange:_____

DATE	BUY @ PRICE	BUY AMOUNT	MIN SELL PT	SELL @ PRICE	SELL AMOUNT	PROFIT/LOSS

COIN/TOKEN:_____ Exchange:_____

DATE	BUY @ PRICE	BUY AMOUNT	MIN SELL PT	SELL @ PRICE	SELL AMOUNT	PROFIT/LOSS

COIN/TOKEN:_____ Exchange:_____

DATE	BUY @ PRICE	BUY AMOUNT	MIN SELL PT	SELL @ PRICE	SELL AMOUNT	PROFIT/LOSS

COIN/TOKEN:_____ Exchange:_____

DATE	BUY @ PRICE	BUY AMOUNT	MIN SELL PT	SELL @ PRICE	SELL AMOUNT	PROFIT/LOSS

COIN/TOKEN:_____ Exchange:_____

DATE	BUY @ PRICE	BUY AMOUNT	MIN SELL PT	SELL @ PRICE	SELL AMOUNT	PROFIT/LOSS

COIN/TOKEN:_____ Exchange:_____

DATE	BUY @ PRICE	BUY AMOUNT	MIN SELL PT	SELL @ PRICE	SELL AMOUNT	PROFIT/LOSS

COIN/TOKEN:_____ Exchange:_____

DATE	BUY @ PRICE	BUY AMOUNT	MIN SELL PT	SELL @ PRICE	SELL AMOUNT	PROFIT/LOSS

COIN/TOKEN:_____ Exchange:_____

DATE	BUY @ PRICE	BUY AMOUNT	MIN SELL PT	SELL @ PRICE	SELL AMOUNT	PROFIT/LOSS

COIN/TOKEN:_____ Exchange:_____

DATE	BUY @ PRICE	BUY AMOUNT	MIN SELL PT	SELL @ PRICE	SELL AMOUNT	PROFIT/LOSS

COIN/TOKEN:_____ Exchange:_____

DATE	BUY @ PRICE	BUY AMOUNT	MIN SELL PT	SELL @ PRICE	SELL AMOUNT	PROFIT/LOSS

COIN/TOKEN:_____ Exchange:_____

DATE	BUY @ PRICE	BUY AMOUNT	MIN SELL PT	SELL @ PRICE	SELL AMOUNT	PROFIT/LOSS

COIN/TOKEN:_____ Exchange:_____

DATE	BUY @ PRICE	BUY AMOUNT	MIN SELL PT	SELL @ PRICE	SELL AMOUNT	PROFIT/LOSS

COIN/TOKEN:_____ Exchange:_____

DATE	BUY @ PRICE	BUY AMOUNT	MIN SELL PT	SELL @ PRICE	SELL AMOUNT	PROFIT/LOSS

COIN/TOKEN:_____ Exchange:_____

DATE	BUY @ PRICE	BUY AMOUNT	MIN SELL PT	SELL @ PRICE	SELL AMOUNT	PROFIT/LOSS

COIN/TOKEN:_____ Exchange:_____

DATE	BUY @ PRICE	BUY AMOUNT	MIN SELL PT	SELL @ PRICE	SELL AMOUNT	PROFIT/LOSS

COIN/TOKEN:_____ Exchange:_____

DATE	BUY @ PRICE	BUY AMOUNT	MIN SELL PT	SELL @ PRICE	SELL AMOUNT	PROFIT/LOSS

COIN/TOKEN:_____ Exchange:_____

DATE	BUY @ PRICE	BUY AMOUNT	MIN SELL PT	SELL @ PRICE	SELL AMOUNT	PROFIT/LOSS

COIN/TOKEN:_____ Exchange:_____

DATE	BUY @ PRICE	BUY AMOUNT	MIN SELL PT	SELL @ PRICE	SELL AMOUNT	PROFIT/LOSS

COIN/TOKEN:_____ Exchange:_____

DATE	BUY @ PRICE	BUY AMOUNT	MIN SELL PT	SELL @ PRICE	SELL AMOUNT	PROFIT/LOSS

COIN/TOKEN:_____ Exchange:_____

DATE	BUY @ PRICE	BUY AMOUNT	MIN SELL PT	SELL @ PRICE	SELL AMOUNT	PROFIT/LOSS

COIN/TOKEN:_____ Exchange:_____

DATE	BUY @ PRICE	BUY AMOUNT	MIN SELL PT	SELL @ PRICE	SELL AMOUNT	PROFIT/LOSS

COIN/TOKEN:_____ Exchange:_____

DATE	BUY @ PRICE	BUY AMOUNT	MIN SELL PT	SELL @ PRICE	SELL AMOUNT	PROFIT/LOSS

COIN/TOKEN:_____ Exchange:_____

DATE	BUY @ PRICE	BUY AMOUNT	MIN SELL PT	SELL @ PRICE	SELL AMOUNT	PROFIT/LOSS

COIN/TOKEN:_____ Exchange:_____

DATE	BUY @ PRICE	BUY AMOUNT	MIN SELL PT	SELL @ PRICE	SELL AMOUNT	PROFIT/LOSS

COIN/TOKEN:_____ Exchange:_____

DATE	BUY @ PRICE	BUY AMOUNT	MIN SELL PT	SELL @ PRICE	SELL AMOUNT	PROFIT/LOSS

COIN/TOKEN:_____ Exchange:_____

DATE	BUY @ PRICE	BUY AMOUNT	MIN SELL PT	SELL @ PRICE	SELL AMOUNT	PROFIT/LOSS

COIN/TOKEN:_____ Exchange:_____

DATE	BUY @ PRICE	BUY AMOUNT	MIN SELL PT	SELL @ PRICE	SELL AMOUNT	PROFIT/LOSS

COIN/TOKEN:_____ Exchange:_____

DATE	BUY @ PRICE	BUY AMOUNT	MIN SELL PT	SELL @ PRICE	SELL AMOUNT	PROFIT/LOSS

COIN/TOKEN:_____ Exchange:_____

DATE	BUY @ PRICE	BUY AMOUNT	MIN SELL PT	SELL @ PRICE	SELL AMOUNT	PROFIT/LOSS

COIN/TOKEN:_____ Exchange:_____

DATE	BUY @ PRICE	BUY AMOUNT	MIN SELL PT	SELL @ PRICE	SELL AMOUNT	PROFIT/LOSS

COIN/TOKEN:_____ Exchange:_____

DATE	BUY @ PRICE	BUY AMOUNT	MIN SELL PT	SELL @ PRICE	SELL AMOUNT	PROFIT/LOSS

COIN/TOKEN:_____ Exchange:_____

DATE	BUY @ PRICE	BUY AMOUNT	MIN SELL PT	SELL @ PRICE	SELL AMOUNT	PROFIT/LOSS

COIN/TOKEN:_____ Exchange:_____

DATE	BUY @ PRICE	BUY AMOUNT	MIN SELL PT	SELL @ PRICE	SELL AMOUNT	PROFIT/LOSS

COIN/TOKEN:_____ Exchange:_____

DATE	BUY @ PRICE	BUY AMOUNT	MIN SELL PT	SELL @ PRICE	SELL AMOUNT	PROFIT/LOSS

COIN/TOKEN:_____ Exchange:_____

DATE	BUY @ PRICE	BUY AMOUNT	MIN SELL PT	SELL @ PRICE	SELL AMOUNT	PROFIT/LOSS

COIN/TOKEN:_____ Exchange:_____

DATE	BUY @ PRICE	BUY AMOUNT	MIN SELL PT	SELL @ PRICE	SELL AMOUNT	PROFIT/LOSS

COIN/TOKEN:_____ Exchange:_____

DATE	BUY @ PRICE	BUY AMOUNT	MIN SELL PT	SELL @ PRICE	SELL AMOUNT	PROFIT/LOSS

COIN/TOKEN:_____ Exchange:_____

DATE	BUY @ PRICE	BUY AMOUNT	MIN SELL PT	SELL @ PRICE	SELL AMOUNT	PROFIT/LOSS

COIN/TOKEN:_____ Exchange:_____

DATE	BUY @ PRICE	BUY AMOUNT	MIN SELL PT	SELL @ PRICE	SELL AMOUNT	PROFIT/LOSS

COIN/TOKEN:_____ Exchange:_____

DATE	BUY @ PRICE	BUY AMOUNT	MIN SELL PT	SELL @ PRICE	SELL AMOUNT	PROFIT/LOSS

COIN/TOKEN:_____ Exchange:_____

DATE	BUY @ PRICE	BUY AMOUNT	MIN SELL PT	SELL @ PRICE	SELL AMOUNT	PROFIT/LOSS

COIN/TOKEN:_____ Exchange:_____

DATE	BUY @ PRICE	BUY AMOUNT	MIN SELL PT	SELL @ PRICE	SELL AMOUNT	PROFIT/LOSS

COIN/TOKEN:_____ Exchange:_____

DATE	BUY @ PRICE	BUY AMOUNT	MIN SELL PT	SELL @ PRICE	SELL AMOUNT	PROFIT/LOSS

COIN/TOKEN:_____ Exchange:_____

DATE	BUY @ PRICE	BUY AMOUNT	MIN SELL PT	SELL @ PRICE	SELL AMOUNT	PROFIT/LOSS

COIN/TOKEN:_____ Exchange:_____

DATE	BUY @ PRICE	BUY AMOUNT	MIN SELL PT	SELL @ PRICE	SELL AMOUNT	PROFIT/LOSS

COIN/TOKEN:_____ Exchange:_____

DATE	BUY @ PRICE	BUY AMOUNT	MIN SELL PT	SELL @ PRICE	SELL AMOUNT	PROFIT/LOSS

COIN/TOKEN:_____ Exchange:_____

DATE	BUY @ PRICE	BUY AMOUNT	MIN SELL PT	SELL @ PRICE	SELL AMOUNT	PROFIT/LOSS

COIN/TOKEN:_____ Exchange:_____

DATE	BUY @ PRICE	BUY AMOUNT	MIN SELL PT	SELL @ PRICE	SELL AMOUNT	PROFIT/LOSS

COIN/TOKEN:_____ Exchange:_____

DATE	BUY @ PRICE	BUY AMOUNT	MIN SELL PT	SELL @ PRICE	SELL AMOUNT	PROFIT/LOSS

COIN/TOKEN:_____ Exchange:_____

DATE	BUY @ PRICE	BUY AMOUNT	MIN SELL PT	SELL @ PRICE	SELL AMOUNT	PROFIT/LOSS

COIN/TOKEN:_____ Exchange:_____

DATE	BUY @ PRICE	BUY AMOUNT	MIN SELL PT	SELL @ PRICE	SELL AMOUNT	PROFIT/LOSS

COIN/TOKEN:_____ Exchange:_____

DATE	BUY @ PRICE	BUY AMOUNT	MIN SELL PT	SELL @ PRICE	SELL AMOUNT	PROFIT/LOSS

COIN/TOKEN:_____ Exchange:_____

DATE	BUY @ PRICE	BUY AMOUNT	MIN SELL PT	SELL @ PRICE	SELL AMOUNT	PROFIT/LOSS

COIN/TOKEN:_____ Exchange:_____

DATE	BUY @ PRICE	BUY AMOUNT	MIN SELL PT	SELL @ PRICE	SELL AMOUNT	PROFIT/LOSS

COIN/TOKEN:_____ Exchange:_____

DATE	BUY @ PRICE	BUY AMOUNT	MIN SELL PT	SELL @ PRICE	SELL AMOUNT	PROFIT/LOSS

COIN/TOKEN:_____ Exchange:_____

DATE	BUY @ PRICE	BUY AMOUNT	MIN SELL PT	SELL @ PRICE	SELL AMOUNT	PROFIT/LOSS

COIN/TOKEN:_____ Exchange:_____

DATE	BUY @ PRICE	BUY AMOUNT	MIN SELL PT	SELL @ PRICE	SELL AMOUNT	PROFIT/LOSS

COIN/TOKEN:_____ Exchange:_____

DATE	BUY @ PRICE	BUY AMOUNT	MIN SELL PT	SELL @ PRICE	SELL AMOUNT	PROFIT/LOSS

COIN/TOKEN:_____ Exchange:_____

DATE	BUY @ PRICE	BUY AMOUNT	MIN SELL PT	SELL @ PRICE	SELL AMOUNT	PROFIT/LOSS

COIN/TOKEN:_____ Exchange:_____

DATE	BUY @ PRICE	BUY AMOUNT	MIN SELL PT	SELL @ PRICE	SELL AMOUNT	PROFIT/LOSS

COIN/TOKEN:_____ Exchange:_____

DATE	BUY @ PRICE	BUY AMOUNT	MIN SELL PT	SELL @ PRICE	SELL AMOUNT	PROFIT/LOSS

COIN/TOKEN:_____ Exchange:_____

DATE	BUY @ PRICE	BUY AMOUNT	MIN SELL PT	SELL @ PRICE	SELL AMOUNT	PROFIT/LOSS

COIN/TOKEN:_____ Exchange:_____

DATE	BUY @ PRICE	BUY AMOUNT	MIN SELL PT	SELL @ PRICE	SELL AMOUNT	PROFIT/LOSS

COIN/TOKEN:_____ Exchange:_____

DATE	BUY @ PRICE	BUY AMOUNT	MIN SELL PT	SELL @ PRICE	SELL AMOUNT	PROFIT/LOSS

COIN/TOKEN:_____ Exchange:_____

DATE	BUY @ PRICE	BUY AMOUNT	MIN SELL PT	SELL @ PRICE	SELL AMOUNT	PROFIT/LOSS

COIN/TOKEN:_____ Exchange:_____

DATE	BUY @ PRICE	BUY AMOUNT	MIN SELL PT	SELL @ PRICE	SELL AMOUNT	PROFIT/LOSS

COIN/TOKEN:_____ Exchange:_____

DATE	BUY @ PRICE	BUY AMOUNT	MIN SELL PT	SELL @ PRICE	SELL AMOUNT	PROFIT/LOSS

COIN/TOKEN:_____ Exchange:_____

DATE	BUY @ PRICE	BUY AMOUNT	MIN SELL PT	SELL @ PRICE	SELL AMOUNT	PROFIT/LOSS

COIN/TOKEN:_____ Exchange:_____

DATE	BUY @ PRICE	BUY AMOUNT	MIN SELL PT	SELL @ PRICE	SELL AMOUNT	PROFIT/LOSS

COIN/TOKEN:_____ Exchange:_____

DATE	BUY @ PRICE	BUY AMOUNT	MIN SELL PT	SELL @ PRICE	SELL AMOUNT	PROFIT/LOSS

COIN/TOKEN:_____ Exchange:_____

DATE	BUY @ PRICE	BUY AMOUNT	MIN SELL PT	SELL @ PRICE	SELL AMOUNT	PROFIT/LOSS

COIN/TOKEN:_____ Exchange:_____

DATE	BUY @ PRICE	BUY AMOUNT	MIN SELL PT	SELL @ PRICE	SELL AMOUNT	PROFIT/LOSS

COIN/TOKEN:_____ Exchange:_____

DATE	BUY @ PRICE	BUY AMOUNT	MIN SELL PT	SELL @ PRICE	SELL AMOUNT	PROFIT/LOSS

COIN/TOKEN:_____ Exchange:_____

DATE	BUY @ PRICE	BUY AMOUNT	MIN SELL PT	SELL @ PRICE	SELL AMOUNT	PROFIT/LOSS

COIN/TOKEN:_____ Exchange:_____

DATE	BUY @ PRICE	BUY AMOUNT	MIN SELL PT	SELL @ PRICE	SELL AMOUNT	PROFIT/LOSS

COIN/TOKEN:_____ Exchange:_____

DATE	BUY @ PRICE	BUY AMOUNT	MIN SELL PT	SELL @ PRICE	SELL AMOUNT	PROFIT/LOSS

COIN/TOKEN:_____ Exchange:_____

DATE	BUY @ PRICE	BUY AMOUNT	MIN SELL PT	SELL @ PRICE	SELL AMOUNT	PROFIT/LOSS

COIN/TOKEN:_____ Exchange:_____

DATE	BUY @ PRICE	BUY AMOUNT	MIN SELL PT	SELL @ PRICE	SELL AMOUNT	PROFIT/LOSS

COIN/TOKEN:_____ Exchange:_____

DATE	BUY @ PRICE	BUY AMOUNT	MIN SELL PT	SELL @ PRICE	SELL AMOUNT	PROFIT/LOSS

COIN/TOKEN:_____ Exchange:_____

DATE	BUY @ PRICE	BUY AMOUNT	MIN SELL PT	SELL @ PRICE	SELL AMOUNT	PROFIT/LOSS

COIN/TOKEN:_____ Exchange:_____

DATE	BUY @ PRICE	BUY AMOUNT	MIN SELL PT	SELL @ PRICE	SELL AMOUNT	PROFIT/LOSS

COIN/TOKEN:_____ Exchange:_____

DATE	BUY @ PRICE	BUY AMOUNT	MIN SELL PT	SELL @ PRICE	SELL AMOUNT	PROFIT/LOSS

COIN/TOKEN:_____ Exchange:_____

DATE	BUY @ PRICE	BUY AMOUNT	MIN SELL PT	SELL @ PRICE	SELL AMOUNT	PROFIT/LOSS

COIN/TOKEN:_____ Exchange:_____

DATE	BUY @ PRICE	BUY AMOUNT	MIN SELL PT	SELL @ PRICE	SELL AMOUNT	PROFIT/LOSS

COIN/TOKEN:_____ Exchange:_____

DATE	BUY @ PRICE	BUY AMOUNT	MIN SELL PT	SELL @ PRICE	SELL AMOUNT	PROFIT/LOSS

COIN/TOKEN:_____ Exchange:_____

DATE	BUY @ PRICE	BUY AMOUNT	MIN SELL PT	SELL @ PRICE	SELL AMOUNT	PROFIT/LOSS

COIN/TOKEN:_____ Exchange:_____

DATE	BUY @ PRICE	BUY AMOUNT	MIN SELL PT	SELL @ PRICE	SELL AMOUNT	PROFIT/LOSS

COIN/TOKEN:_____ Exchange:_____

DATE	BUY @ PRICE	BUY AMOUNT	MIN SELL PT	SELL @ PRICE	SELL AMOUNT	PROFIT/LOSS

COIN/TOKEN:_____ Exchange:_____

DATE	BUY @ PRICE	BUY AMOUNT	MIN SELL PT	SELL @ PRICE	SELL AMOUNT	PROFIT/LOSS

COIN/TOKEN:_____ Exchange:_____

DATE	BUY @ PRICE	BUY AMOUNT	MIN SELL PT	SELL @ PRICE	SELL AMOUNT	PROFIT/LOSS

COIN/TOKEN:_____ Exchange:_____

DATE	BUY @ PRICE	BUY AMOUNT	MIN SELL PT	SELL @ PRICE	SELL AMOUNT	PROFIT/LOSS

COIN/TOKEN:_____ Exchange:_____

DATE	BUY @ PRICE	BUY AMOUNT	MIN SELL PT	SELL @ PRICE	SELL AMOUNT	PROFIT/LOSS

COIN/TOKEN:_____ Exchange:_____

DATE	BUY @ PRICE	BUY AMOUNT	MIN SELL PT	SELL @ PRICE	SELL AMOUNT	PROFIT/LOSS

COIN/TOKEN:_____ Exchange:_____

DATE	BUY @ PRICE	BUY AMOUNT	MIN SELL PT	SELL @ PRICE	SELL AMOUNT	PROFIT/LOSS

COIN/TOKEN:_____ Exchange:_____

DATE	BUY @ PRICE	BUY AMOUNT	MIN SELL PT	SELL @ PRICE	SELL AMOUNT	PROFIT/LOSS

COIN/TOKEN:_____ Exchange:_____

DATE	BUY @ PRICE	BUY AMOUNT	MIN SELL PT	SELL @ PRICE	SELL AMOUNT	PROFIT/LOSS

COIN/TOKEN:_____ Exchange:_____

DATE	BUY @ PRICE	BUY AMOUNT	MIN SELL PT	SELL @ PRICE	SELL AMOUNT	PROFIT/LOSS

COIN/TOKEN:_____ Exchange:_____

DATE	BUY @ PRICE	BUY AMOUNT	MIN SELL PT	SELL @ PRICE	SELL AMOUNT	PROFIT/LOSS

COIN/TOKEN:_____ Exchange:_____

DATE	BUY @ PRICE	BUY AMOUNT	MIN SELL PT	SELL @ PRICE	SELL AMOUNT	PROFIT/LOSS

COIN/TOKEN:_____ Exchange:_____

DATE	BUY @ PRICE	BUY AMOUNT	MIN SELL PT	SELL @ PRICE	SELL AMOUNT	PROFIT/LOSS

COIN/TOKEN:_____ Exchange:_____

DATE	BUY @ PRICE	BUY AMOUNT	MIN SELL PT	SELL @ PRICE	SELL AMOUNT	PROFIT/LOSS

COIN/TOKEN:_____ Exchange:_____

DATE	BUY @ PRICE	BUY AMOUNT	MIN SELL PT	SELL @ PRICE	SELL AMOUNT	PROFIT/LOSS

COIN/TOKEN:_____ Exchange:_____

DATE	BUY @ PRICE	BUY AMOUNT	MIN SELL PT	SELL @ PRICE	SELL AMOUNT	PROFIT/LOSS

COIN/TOKEN:_____ Exchange:_____

DATE	BUY @ PRICE	BUY AMOUNT	MIN SELL PT	SELL @ PRICE	SELL AMOUNT	PROFIT/LOSS

COIN/TOKEN:_____ Exchange:_____

DATE	BUY @ PRICE	BUY AMOUNT	MIN SELL PT	SELL @ PRICE	SELL AMOUNT	PROFIT/LOSS

COIN/TOKEN:_____ Exchange:_____

DATE	BUY @ PRICE	BUY AMOUNT	MIN SELL PT	SELL @ PRICE	SELL AMOUNT	PROFIT/LOSS

COIN/TOKEN:_____ Exchange:_____

DATE	BUY @ PRICE	BUY AMOUNT	MIN SELL PT	SELL @ PRICE	SELL AMOUNT	PROFIT/LOSS

COIN/TOKEN:_____ Exchange:_____

DATE	BUY @ PRICE	BUY AMOUNT	MIN SELL PT	SELL @ PRICE	SELL AMOUNT	PROFIT/LOSS

COIN/TOKEN:_____ Exchange:_____

DATE	BUY @ PRICE	BUY AMOUNT	MIN SELL PT	SELL @ PRICE	SELL AMOUNT	PROFIT/LOSS

COIN/TOKEN:_____ Exchange:_____

DATE	BUY @ PRICE	BUY AMOUNT	MIN SELL PT	SELL @ PRICE	SELL AMOUNT	PROFIT/LOSS

COIN/TOKEN:_____ Exchange:_____

DATE	BUY @ PRICE	BUY AMOUNT	MIN SELL PT	SELL @ PRICE	SELL AMOUNT	PROFIT/LOSS

COIN/TOKEN:_____ Exchange:_____

DATE	BUY @ PRICE	BUY AMOUNT	MIN SELL PT	SELL @ PRICE	SELL AMOUNT	PROFIT/LOSS

COIN/TOKEN:_____ Exchange:_____

DATE	BUY @ PRICE	BUY AMOUNT	MIN SELL PT	SELL @ PRICE	SELL AMOUNT	PROFIT/LOSS

COIN/TOKEN:_____ Exchange:_____

DATE	BUY @ PRICE	BUY AMOUNT	MIN SELL PT	SELL @ PRICE	SELL AMOUNT	PROFIT/LOSS

COIN/TOKEN:_____ Exchange:_____

DATE	BUY @ PRICE	BUY AMOUNT	MIN SELL PT	SELL @ PRICE	SELL AMOUNT	PROFIT/LOSS

COIN/TOKEN:_____ Exchange:_____

DATE	BUY @ PRICE	BUY AMOUNT	MIN SELL PT	SELL @ PRICE	SELL AMOUNT	PROFIT/LOSS

COIN/TOKEN:_____ Exchange:_____

DATE	BUY @ PRICE	BUY AMOUNT	MIN SELL PT	SELL @ PRICE	SELL AMOUNT	PROFIT/LOSS

COIN/TOKEN:_____ Exchange:_____

DATE	BUY @ PRICE	BUY AMOUNT	MIN SELL PT	SELL @ PRICE	SELL AMOUNT	PROFIT/LOSS

COIN/TOKEN:_____ Exchange:_____

DATE	BUY @ PRICE	BUY AMOUNT	MIN SELL PT	SELL @ PRICE	SELL AMOUNT	PROFIT/LOSS

COIN/TOKEN:_____ Exchange:_____

DATE	BUY @ PRICE	BUY AMOUNT	MIN SELL PT	SELL @ PRICE	SELL AMOUNT	PROFIT/LOSS

COIN/TOKEN:_____ Exchange:_____

DATE	BUY @ PRICE	BUY AMOUNT	MIN SELL PT	SELL @ PRICE	SELL AMOUNT	PROFIT/LOSS

COIN/TOKEN:_____ Exchange:_____

DATE	BUY @ PRICE	BUY AMOUNT	MIN SELL PT	SELL @ PRICE	SELL AMOUNT	PROFIT/LOSS

COIN/TOKEN:_____ Exchange:_____

DATE	BUY @ PRICE	BUY AMOUNT	MIN SELL PT	SELL @ PRICE	SELL AMOUNT	PROFIT/LOSS

COIN/TOKEN:_____ Exchange:_____

DATE	BUY @ PRICE	BUY AMOUNT	MIN SELL PT	SELL @ PRICE	SELL AMOUNT	PROFIT/LOSS